P9-BZR-310

SCIENCE MISSIONS

Mission to Mars

Eve Hartman and Wendy Meshbesher

Chicago, Illinois

Edited by Adam Miller, Andrew Farrow, and Adrian Vigliano
Designed by Philippa Jenkins
Original illustrations © Capstone Global Library Ltd.
Illustrated by KJA-artists.com
Picture research by Tracy Cummins
Production by Alison Parsons
Originated by Dot Gradations
Printed and bound in China by South China Printing Company Ltd

14 13 12 11 10
10 9 8 7 6 5 4 3 2 1

Library of Congress Cataloging-in-Publication Data
Hartman, Eve.
Mission to Mars / Eve Hartman and Wendy Meshbesher.
p. cm. — (Science Missions)
Includes bibliographical references and index.
ISBN 978-1-4109-3821-3 (hc)
1. Space flight to Mars—Juvenile literature.
2. Mars (Planet)—Exploration—Juvenile literature.
3. Mars probes—Juvenile literature.
4. Astranautics—Juvenile literature.
I. Meshbesher, Wendy. II. Title.
TL799.M3H37 2011
629.45'53—dc22

2009053209

Acknowledgments
The author and publishers are grateful to the following for permission to reproduce copyright material: Alamy ©Photo12 **p.17**; Alamy ©B.A.E. Inc. **pp.48&49**; Corbis ©Joel W. Rogers **p.6**; Corbis ©Underwood & Underwood **p.22**; Corbis ©Roger Ressmeyer/NASA **p.32**; Corbis ©SPACE BIOSPHERES VENTURES **p.43 top**; Corbis ©Bettmann **p.46**; Corbis ©Craig Aurness **p.47**; Getty Images/ROBERT SULLIVAN **p.23**; Getty Images/VisionsofAmerica/Joe Sohm **p.43**; NASA/JPL/USGS **pp.4&5**; NASA/JPL/Cornell University/Maas Digital **p.8**; NASA/JPL-Caltech/Cornel **p.10**; NASA/JPL **pp.12&13**; NASA/JPL **p.14**; NASA/HQ-GRIN **p.16**; NASA/JPL/USGS **p.18**; NASA/JPL **p.19**; NASA **pp.20&21**; NASA/Kennedy Space Center (NASA-KSC) **p.27**; NASA-HQ/GRIN **p.29**; NASA/Kennedy Space Center **p.33**; NASA **p.35**; NASA/Bill Stafford **p.37**; NASA **p.38**; NASA **p.39**; NASA-HQ/GRIN **pp.30&31**; Photo Researchers, Inc./Ed Young **p.7**; Photo Researchers, Inc./Shigemi Numazawa/Atlas Photo Bank **pp.40&41**; Shutterstock ©Daniela Sachsenheimer **p.24**; Shutterstock/Walter S. Becker **p.34**; Shutterstock/Khoo Si Lin **p.44**; Shutterstock/Maksim Shmeljov **pp.50&51**.

Cover photograph of the Phoenix Mission lander reproduced with the permission of NASA/JPL.

The authors thank Gordon Green for his enthusiasm and support.

The publishers would like to thank Geza Gyuk for his invaluable help in the preparation of this book.

CONTENTS

Some words are printed in bold, **like this**. You can find out what they mean by looking in the glossary. You can also look out for them in the **WORD STORE** box at the bottom of each page.

MISSION TO MARS

"What we need is a destination in space that offers great rewards for the risks to achieve it. I believe that destination must be homesteading Mars, the first human colony on another world."

Buzz Aldrin, former astronaut

On July 20, 1969, astronauts Neil Armstrong and Edwin "Buzz" Aldrin became the first humans to walk on the Moon. Over the next few years, astronauts landed on the Moon six more times. Then, Moon exploration stopped.

Today, some scientists are calling for a return to the Moon. Certainly much remains to be discovered there. But Aldrin, now a private citizen, suggests a new mission—a mission to the planet Mars.

Mars is much farther away from Earth than the Moon. Traveling to and from Mars would present a huge number of challenges, as well as risks. Yet Aldrin argues that humans are explorers and pioneers, and that Mars is now the next destination that we should reach.

Mars has already been explored with robotic **probes** and **rovers**. Now U.S. National Aeronautics and Space Administration (**NASA**) scientists, along with government leaders and private citizens, are seriously considering sending astronauts there, perhaps by the year 2037. Someday, maybe a human colony will be established on Mars.

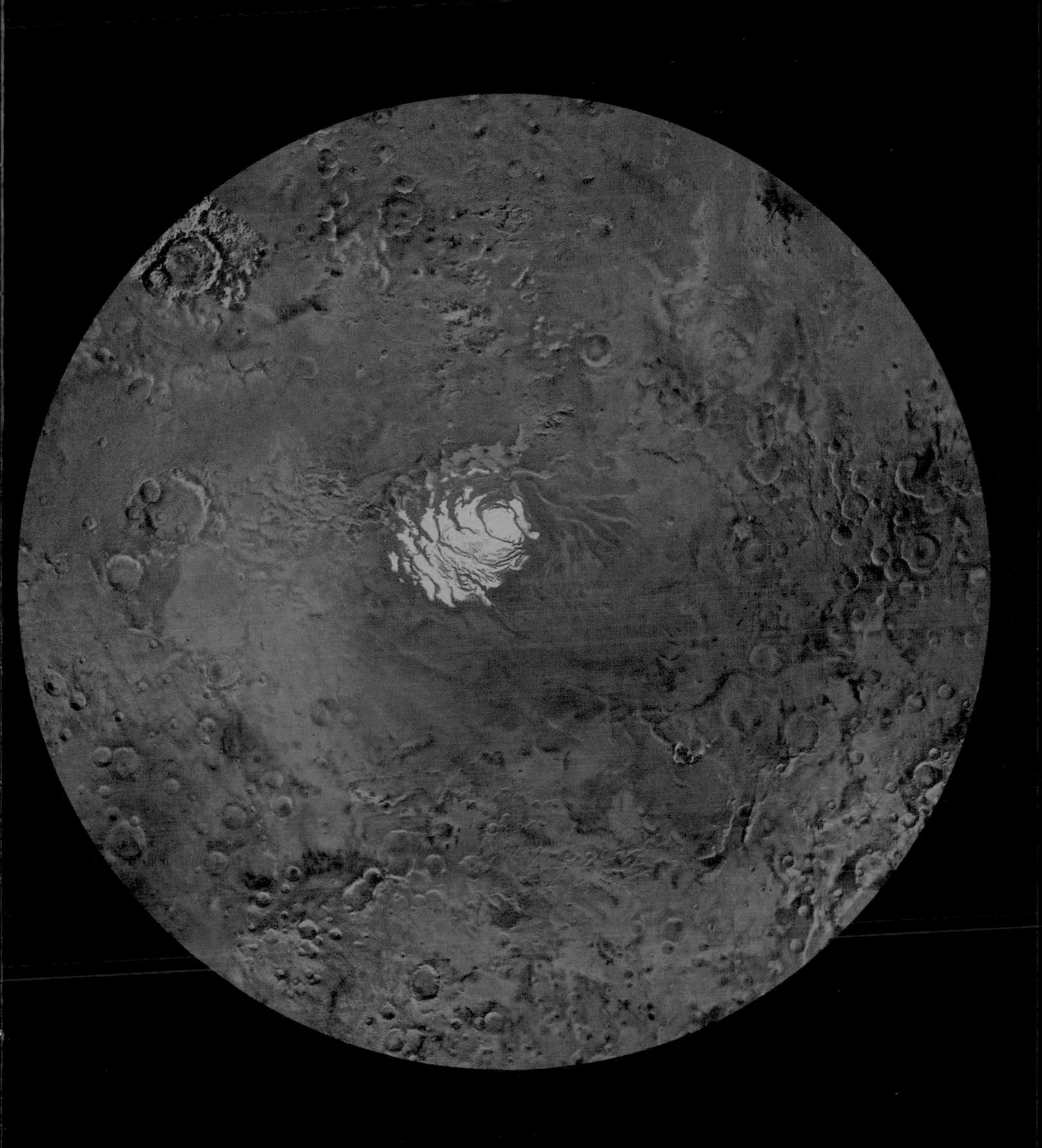

The surface of Mars's southern polar plain. The lightly colored area in the center is Mars's southern ice cap. There is also a much larger ice cap on the northern pole.

Journeys of the past

Humans have been exploring the world around them long before space exploration became possible. In many ways the world we live in today is a result of explorations.

The first humans lived millions of years ago in Africa. From there they spread to places all across Earth. Much later, when Europeans began exploring other continents, they discovered human civilizations wherever they went.

Traveling across the world was both slow and dangerous. Marco Polo, an Italian merchant, traveled from Italy to Asia over land in the 1200s. His journey took 24 years. Later, explorers sailed ships on the oceans. In 1519 Portuguese explorer Ferdinand Magellan and a crew of over 200 sailors began a journey around the world. The journey took three years and claimed the lives of most of the sailors, including Magellan himself. In the late 1500s, English explorer Francis Drake survived his round-the-world trip, but he was almost murdered by his crew.

Francis Drake took three years to sail around the world. The photo shows a modern recreation of his ship, the Golden Hinde.

WORD STORE **climate** yearly pattern of weather

The explorer's life

To find their way, early explorers and navigators relied on the objects they saw in the sky. They knew that the Sun rose in the eastern sky, climbed higher during the day, then set to the west. At night the constellations appeared. Constellations are patterns of stars in the sky.

This instrument, called a sextant, helped explorers find their way by using the stars.

Imagine yourself on an ocean journey with Magellan or Drake. You would be far from home, with only the stars and the Sun to guide you. Your life would depend entirely on your ship, which you would use to carry all your food and drinking water. You might feel a little scared or anxious, but also excited and thrilled. You would be in the middle of a grand adventure, a journey to a place none of your fellow citizens had ever visited.

For the same reasons, an astronaut on a mission to Mars might feel just this way. Yet, as you will discover, we already know a great deal about Mars. When astronauts board a spaceship for Mars, they already will be very familiar with their destination.

GOALS FOR MARS EXPLORATION

All of NASA's missions to Mars are designed to meet these four goals:

Goal 1: Determine if life ever arose on Mars

Goal 2: Learn about the climate of Mars

Goal 3: Investigate the geology of Mars

Goal 4: Prepare for human exploration of Mars

WORD STORE **geology** science of studying physical structures, such as planets

Space probes to Mars

NASA began its Mars exploration program in the 1960s. Since then, other countries have sent space probes to explore Mars, and more missions are planned for the future. A space probe is a spaceship that carries cameras and other instruments, but does not carry astronauts. Probes use radio waves to communicate with scientists on Earth.

The following is an overview of several of the space probes that have explored Mars.

Mariner missions: 1960s

In 1965 NASA's Mariner 4 became the first spacecraft to approach Mars and send photographs of the planet to Earth. A few years later, Mariner 9 became the first spacecraft to **orbit** Mars. The Mariner missions showed that Mars had a varied surface that included huge volcanoes, steep canyons, and evidence of wind erosion. The missions also measured the atmospheric pressure, or weight of the air above the surface. It proved to be a small fraction of the air pressure on Earth.

Project Viking: 1970s

Project Viking succeeded in landing on the Martian surface (the surface of Mars). Two spacecraft, named Viking 1 and Viking 2, each consisted of an orbiter and lander. The landers carried instruments that measured the Martian soil, **atmosphere**, and temperature. The instruments also tested for signs of water and of life, which they did not find.

NASA's Mars Exploration Rover.

WORD STORE **atmosphere** layer of gases surrounding a planet

CLOSE NEIGHBORS?

Earth is the third planet from the Sun, and Mars is the fourth. But that does not make them close neighbors all the time. The reason is that the two planets orbit the Sun at different speeds. The distance between them can be as close as 55 million kilometers (34 million miles) or 8 times as far!

All missions to Mars are planned to use the orbits of both planets to help save energy on the trip. This is because, when less energy is used in travel, the spacecraft can carry more equipment to use on Mars. But doing this sometimes means taking a longer route from Earth to Mars.

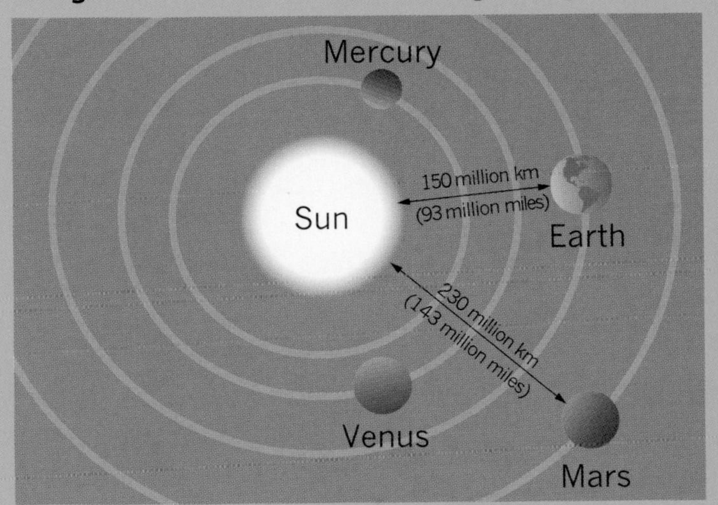

A good plan for traveling from Earth to Mars has to make use of the orbits of both planets.

Mars Pathfinder: 1990s

The Mars Pathfinder mission included the first rover to successfully explore Mars. A rover is like a robotic car. The rover from Pathfinder carried a computer and many instruments to study soil and rock samples. The Mars Pathfinder cost about one-fifteenth as much as a Viking mission.

Mars Express: 2000s

In 2003 the European Space Agency (ESA) launched a space probe called the Mars Express. The probe carried a lander that did not function as planned. But the orbiter proved successful. It has been using sensitive cameras, radio waves, and other technology to map the Martian surface and study its atmosphere.

The orbiter discovered ice in a polar region on the surface. It also discovered small amounts of ammonia and methane in the atmosphere. These gases could be signs of living things or of activity in the planet's interior.

WORD STORE **orbit** to circle around something

More probes

Space probes continue to explore Mars, and new probes will be launched in the years to come. The following are some recent missions.

Spirit and *Opportunity*

Since 2004 two rovers, named *Spirit* and *Opportunity*, have been exploring the Martian surface. The rovers are so advanced that they have been called robot scientists. Both carry a wide variety of instruments for testing the Martian soil and air. They can even pick up a rock, scrape its surface, and study the material underneath.

Spirit and *Opportunity* have been conducting very sensitive tests for signs of life. However, the tests have not provided clear answers. The rovers discovered chemicals in the Martian soil that could have been made by living things. But they could also have been made by other processes.

If you could ride on the Spirit rover, this is what you might see. Photos from probes confirm that Mars is a reddish rocky planet.

WORD STORE **mineral** nonliving metal or other nonliving material

SUCCESS!

Many missions to Mars were not successful. Yet other missions provided more data and lasted longer than their creators had ever hoped for. *Spirit* and *Opportunity* were expected to roam across Mars and send data for only a few months. Instead they did this for many years. Not many machines do their jobs so well for so long—especially not without visits from a mechanic!

Mars Reconnaissance Orbiter

The Mars Reconnaissance Orbiter acts somewhat like a weather satellite. It carries cameras and **radar** to study the Martian atmosphere and surface conditions. These cameras have provided the best images yet of the Martian surface. But the orbiter's most useful function is in communication. Future missions to Mars will use the orbiter's radio transmitters to relay messages to and from Earth.

Mars Scout program

In the Mars Scout program, NASA is sending small, relatively inexpensive space probes to Mars. The first mission was the Phoenix probe, which landed near the northern ice cap of Mars in 2008. Its goal was to search for traces of liquid water in the soil, as well as signs of life.

Dr. Peter Smith summed up the results: "Not only did we find water ice, as expected, but the soil chemistry and **minerals** we observed lead us to believe this site had a wetter and warmer climate in the recent past—the last few million years—and could again in the future."

The MAVEN space probe will be the next mission of the Mars Scout program. It will study the gases of the Martian atmosphere.

What next?

In the future NASA and other space agencies plan to send more probes to Mars. They hope to explore above the surface with probes that can fly, much like airplanes. They hope to explore below the surface with probes that can dig. One proposal is for a Mars sample return mission, which would gather soil and rock samples and return them to Earth.

Why keep returning to Mars? One reason is to answer questions that the previous missions raised. What happened to the liquid water that Mars had in its past? What is making the ammonia and methane gases in the Martian atmosphere? Did life exist on Mars in its distant past? If so, what happened to it?

WORD STORE **radar** system for detecting objects using electromagnetic waves

MEET OUR NEIGHBOR

What if you opened your bedroom window one morning and saw this view? Would you still want to head out your front door? If so, be sure to wear warm clothes. The average temperature on Mars is a chilly –63°C (–81°F). This is about as cold as winter in the continent of Antarctica, back on Earth.

You will also need to bring the gas **oxygen** with you, as well as liquid water to drink. Mars has very little oxygen and liquid water, which means Earth-like living things cannot survive there. At least your supplies should be easy to carry. The force of gravity on Mars is three-eighths its force on Earth.

Mars is smaller than Earth—about half as large in **radius** and one-tenth as large in mass. But Mars is Earth's neighbor in space and is similar in many ways. Both have rocky surfaces, and both have at least one moon in **orbit** around them. Mars has two moons, named Phobos and Deimos.

In other ways, however, Earth and Mars are extremely different. The photo only begins to explain why.

This Martian landscape was photographed during NASA's Pathfinder mission, southwest of the mission's landing site.

Structure of Mars

As space **probes** have shown, the structure of Mars is much like that of Earth. The planet is rocky and is surrounded by an **atmosphere**. Yet the surface of Mars lacks liquid water, which may be its most important difference from Earth.

Surface and interior

The rocks of Mars have a reddish color. This comes from a red compound called iron oxide, also known as rust.

The surface of Mars has many features, including craters, steep canyons, and valleys. Mars also has the largest volcanoes in the solar system. The volcano Olympus Mons is so large it can be viewed from Earth with a simple telescope. It is three times higher than Mount Everest, the tallest mountain on Earth. Volcanoes erupt when hot, melted rock escapes from the interior onto the crust. The crust is the rocky surface of a planet.

The Viking 1 Orbiter took this photo of Olympus Mons. The volcano is over 600 kilometers (370 miles) wide.

WORD STORE

magnetic field effect of a magnet in the region around it

nitrogen gas in Earth's atmosphere that is used by living things

On Earth, volcanoes form in different regions over time. This happens because Earth's crust slowly moves. On Mars the giant volcanoes show that the crust does not move. Beginning soon after the planet formed, the Mars volcanoes kept erupting in the same spots. They grew huge!

Mars versus Earth

Here are some basic differences between Mars and Earth.

	MARS	EARTH
Average distance from Sun	230 million kilometers (almost 143 million miles)	150 million kilometers (over 93 million miles)
Length of year	687 Earth days	365.25 Earth days
Surface	rocky; little water	oceans and continents with much water
Atmosphere	thin; mostly carbon dioxide	thick; mostly nitrogen and oxygen
Number of moons	2	1

Atmosphere

The atmosphere on Mars is made mostly of the gas carbon dioxide. Other gases include **nitrogen** and very small amounts of oxygen and water vapor. The atmosphere is also very thin. The air pressure on the surface of Mars is about one percent of the air pressure on Earth.

One reason why Mars has such a thin atmosphere is because it lost its **magnetic field**. Earth has a magnetic field, which is why magnetic compasses point north. Earth's magnetism deflects the **solar wind**, which is a stream of electrons and other **particles** from the Sun. When Mars lost its magnetic field, the solar wind began stripping away gases from its atmosphere.

Water

Mars has a lot of water, but nearly all of it is frozen. Ice caps cover the north and south poles of Mars, much like the way they cover Earth's poles. Parts of Martian soil also are filled with ice, like tundra. Tundra is ground that has a permanently frozen layer below the surface.

Liquid water cannot exist on the surface of Mars today—at least not for longer than a few moments. Because Mars has a hot interior, however, it might exist below the surface. Evidence also suggests that bodies of water might have covered Mars in the past, when its atmosphere was thicker.

WORD STORE

particle tiny piece of material
solar wind particles from the Sun that travel through space

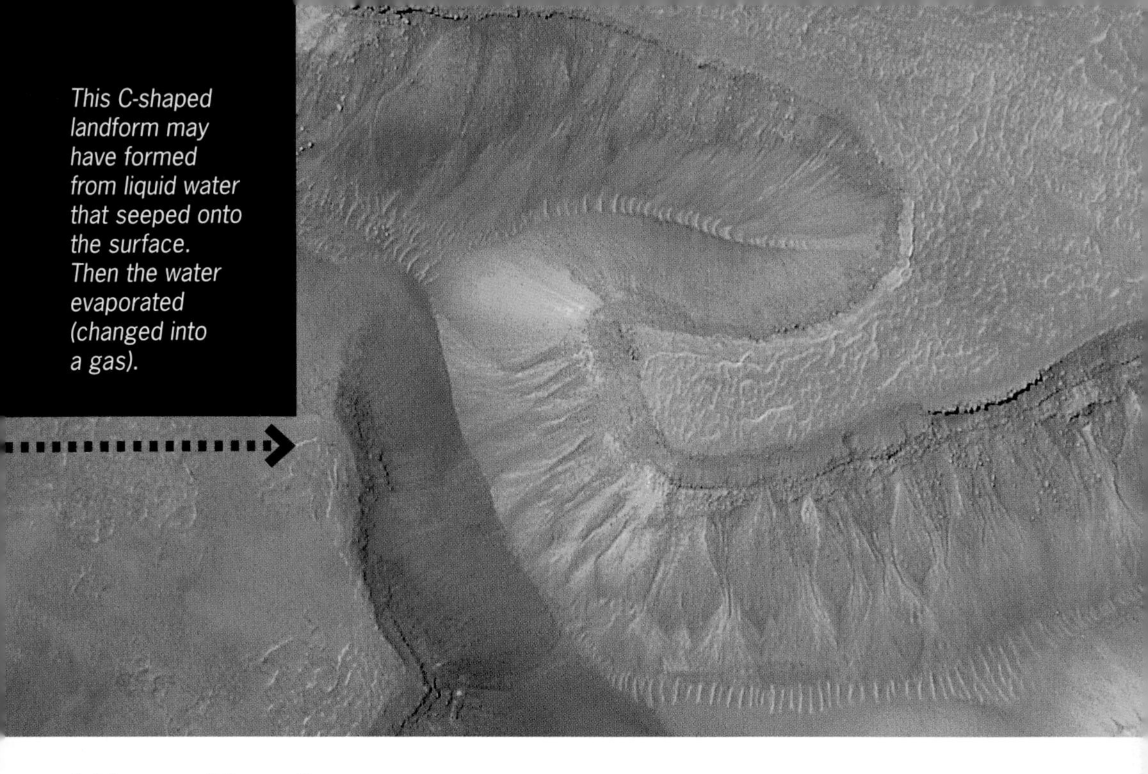

This C-shaped landform may have formed from liquid water that seeped onto the surface. Then the water evaporated (changed into a gas).

Life on Mars?

Does surface life now exist on Mars? After many years of exploration with probes, scientists are fairly certain that the answer is no. The apparent lack of liquid water is the main reason.

On Earth, all living things depend on liquid water. Life flourishes in oceans, rain forests, river valleys, and other places where liquid water collects. Life does not thrive in the Sahara Desert or in Antarctica, where liquid water is absent.

But did surface life ever exist on Mars in the past? This is a more complicated question. Data from the **rovers** *Spirit* and *Opportunity* (see page 10) suggest that water affected the rocks. The rovers also found chemicals that living things could have made. Those living things would have been very simple, much like **bacteria** on Earth.

As of now, however, scientists do not have enough evidence to draw useful conclusions. Life might have existed on Mars, or it might not have. And no one knows if bacteria or similar organisms are alive beneath the surface.

One of the goals of **NASA's** Mars exploration program is to search for evidence of life there. They are designing new probes specifically to help answer this question. If astronauts ever travel to Mars, part of their mission will be to determine if the surface of Mars ever held life. And if that life existed, they will try to find out what happened to it.

WORD STORE

bacteria tiny, single-celled organisms
rover vehicle that roams across a planet's surface

INVASION FROM MARS?

Mars was named after the Roman god of war. Perhaps its red color reminded people of war and violence. For whatever reason, people have often imagined Mars as a violent place.

Many science fiction stories involve creatures from Mars invading Earth. One of the most famous of these stories is *The War of the Worlds* (1898), by the English author H. G. Wells. In 1938 a version of this story was broadcast over the radio. Thousands of listeners thought the events were really happening! Many of them fled their homes, hid in basements, or gathered firearms to defend themselves.

In reality, if life ever existed on Mars, it is unlikely that it was a threat to Earth. Scientists have only found evidence for the possibility of very small and simple living things. They were not as complex as even an earthworm.

Martians invading Earth was a popular theme of movies of the 1950s.

Why not Venus?

The first four planets from the Sun are Mercury, Venus, Earth, and Mars. Mercury is very close to the Sun, and no one thinks that life exists there. But what about Venus, which is Earth's other close neighbor? At their closest points, Venus is even closer to Earth than Mars is. Why aren't we thinking about sending astronauts to Venus?

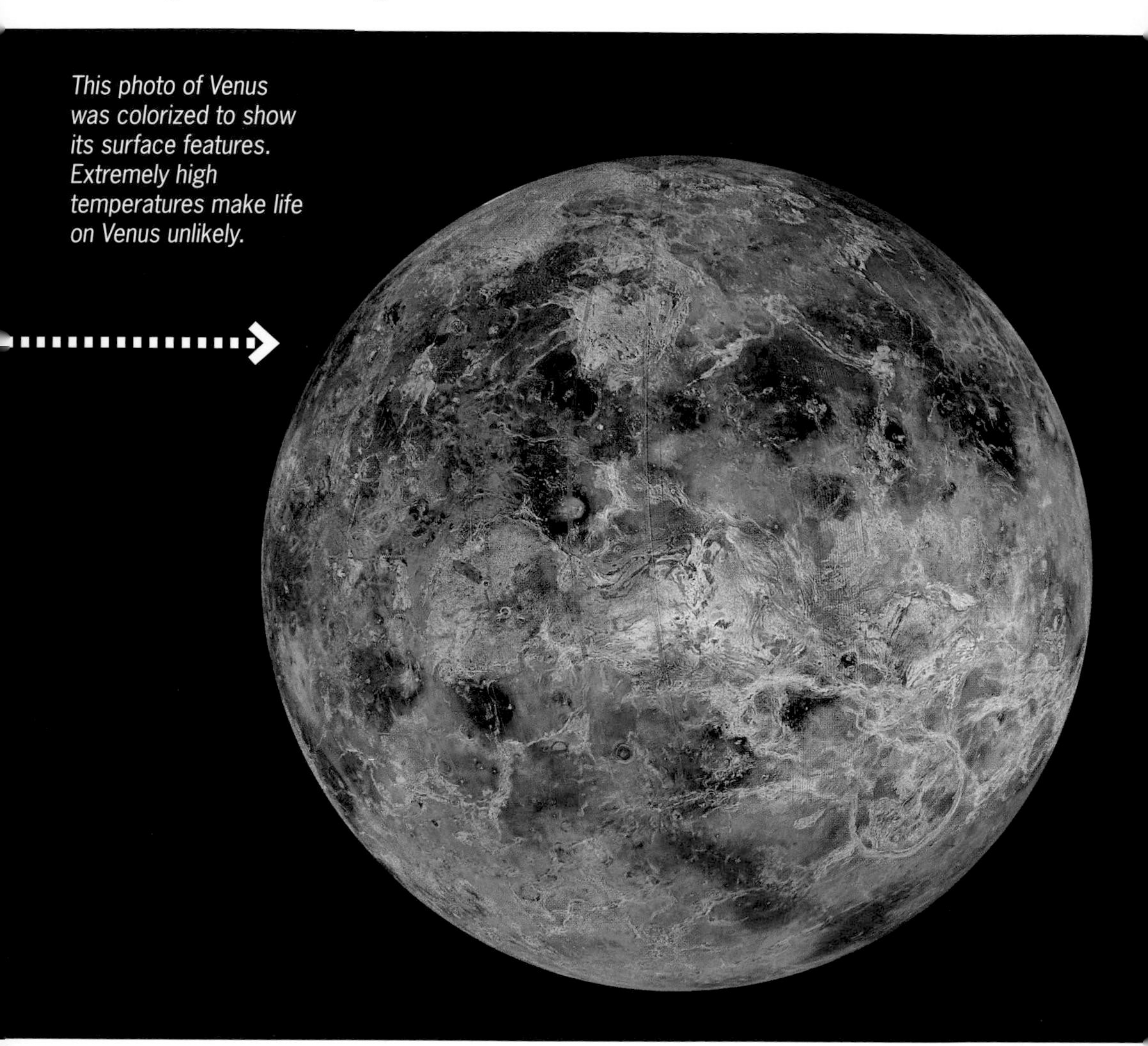

This photo of Venus was colorized to show its surface features. Extremely high temperatures make life on Venus unlikely.

Scientists once thought that Venus might be a lot like Earth. The two planets have about the same size, mass, and chemical makeup. In fact, Venus was once described as Earth's twin! Then, beginning in the 1960s, NASA and other space agencies began sending probes to Venus. Data from these probes showed that if Venus and Earth ever had been twins, they were now very different.

The atmosphere of Venus is very thick, and the average temperature is 457°C (855°F). The air pressure on the surface is about 90 times the air pressure on Earth, which means that the air's weight would crush most Earth-like organisms underneath it. Some Earth organisms, such as certain bacteria, could survive this pressure. But they could never survive the extreme heat. The skies of Venus are not only cloudy, but the clouds are also made of sulfuric acid. On Earth, even a tiny amount of sulfuric acid in rainwater can eat away at a marble statue!

Yet data also suggests that Venus was very different in its past. Venus may have once been much cooler and may have even had liquid water oceans on its surface. Over time, however, the water evaporated and collected in the atmosphere as water vapor. Water vapor is a greenhouse gas, which means it helps trap heat in the air. The water vapor caused air temperatures to rise on Venus, which caused more liquid water to evaporate, which in turn raised temperatures even higher. Eventually all the water evaporated or boiled away.

By studying Venus and Mars, scientists have come to appreciate how perfect Earth is for life. If Earth were even slightly closer to the Sun, more of its liquid water would evaporate. Earth would become more like Venus. If Earth were slightly farther away from the Sun, more of its water would freeze. Earth would become more like Mars.

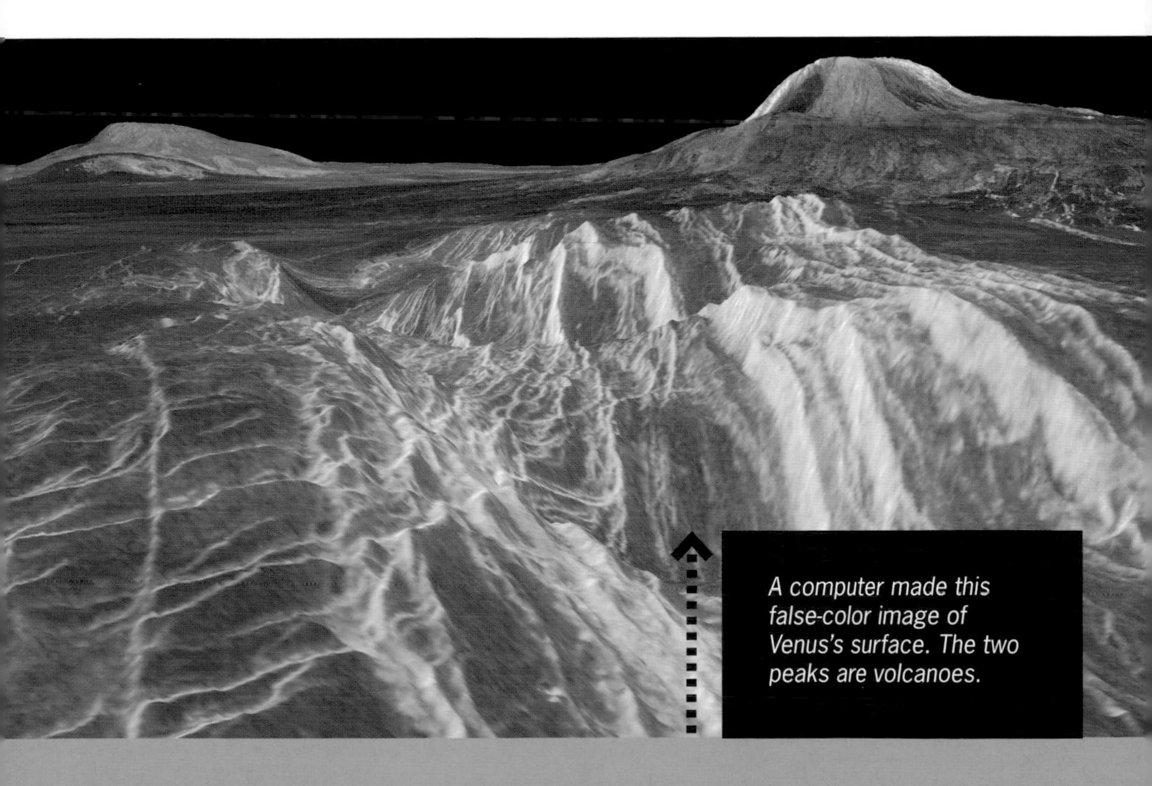

A computer made this false-color image of Venus's surface. The two peaks are volcanoes.

ROCKET SCIENCE

If you throw a baseball up into the sky, gravity will quickly bring it back down. A hot-air balloon and an airplane can stay up in the air for many hours, but they, too, will come down eventually. They also depend on the air to keep them above ground. They cannot travel into space, where there is no air.

It is not easy to leave Earth. But since the 1940s, many rockets have been used to launch objects into space. All have required an enormous amount of fuel.

In the photo on this page, a small space capsule sits on top of the rocket. The rocket will separate from the capsule in stages. Each stage separates from the capsule after all its fuel is burned. Only the capsule will enter space. The stages of the rocket fall to Earth after their work is done.

The rocket being tested in this photo is the Ares 1-X. This rocket was a test vehicle built specifically to carry crew and cargo beyond Earth's **orbit**. An even larger rocket, called the Ares V, is now being designed.

Lindbergh arrived in Paris with little fuel to spare. A spacecraft to Mars must also carry enough fuel for its journey.

The need for fuel

In 1927 U.S. pilot Charles Lindbergh amazed people everywhere by flying a small airplane nonstop across the Atlantic Ocean. But why was his achievement so impressive? One reason is because an airplane can hold only a limited amount of fuel. Lindbergh succeeded because his plane carried a huge amount of fuel and very little else. He left behind things he thought were too heavy—including a radio and a parachute!

Like Lindbergh's airplane, a rocket is also designed to hold as much fuel as possible for its size.

A fuel is a substance that can release energy. Typically, the energy is released by burning, which is a chemical reaction with **oxygen**. Ordinary fuels include wood, coal, natural gas, and gasoline. Each of these fuels combine with oxygen to release energy, often in the form of heat and light.

WORD STORE

hydrogen chemical used as a fuel when in liquid form
oxygen gas in Earth's atmosphere that certain organisms need

Rocket fuel

What is the best fuel to power a rocket? Ordinary gasoline burns too slowly and poorly to be effective. So do natural gas, propane, and even the fuel that jets use. Instead, some rockets use **hydrogen** as a fuel. Hydrogen and oxygen react to release a huge amount of energy. The reaction produces water and no by-products.

Because rocket fuel must burn very quickly, a rocket is loaded with both hydrogen and oxygen. They are loaded in the liquid state, which makes them easier to carry. Many rockets also use forms of solid fuel.

Mars rockets have often used different combinations of fuels, such as solid rocket boosters for the first stage and liquid hydrogen and oxygen for the second stage. These fuels have helped send space **probes** to Mars and beyond. But sending astronauts to Mars would take much more fuel than ever used before. This is because the astronauts need to return home.

Liquid hydrogen combines with oxygen in an explosive reaction.

URANIUM FOR ROCKETS?

Some scientists argue that uranium should be the fuel of choice for long-distance space travel. Uranium now powers large submarines, which often spend months underwater. In theory, a small amount of uranium could replace the huge supplies of rocket fuel now in use.

But there are several problems with this plan. One is that uranium is radioactive, meaning it releases dangerous radiation. Safety questions must be answered before uranium is used as rocket fuel.

WORD STORE

probe unmanned spacecraft that studies with equipment
radiation energy given off by atoms

Pushing down, moving up

Why does a rocket lift off the ground? The forces are much like those that lift a mountain climber up the side of a mountain. Both mountain climbing and a rocket launch are examples of Newton's third law of motion. Named after Isaac Newton, the English scientist who discovered it, the law states that every action force creates an equal but opposite reaction force.

To climb a rock face, a climber pushes down against a rock. This is called the action force. At the same time, the rock pushes upward against the foot. This is the reaction force, and it lifts the body upward. The greater the action force of the feet, the greater the reaction force that lifts the climber up the rock face. You can demonstrate the same principle by climbing a staircase.

The climber's shoe pushes down on the rocky ledge. The downward force pushes the climber up.

Fire!

When a rocket that is fueled by hydrogen and oxygen is fired, the fuel elements combine to form water vapor. The water vapor shoots quickly out of the bottom of the rocket. The flames and billowing clouds that are produced in the rocket launch form from the very hot water vapor that the rocket engines release.

WORD STORE **NASA** U.S. government agency that explores space

The force of the water vapor is the action force, and it points downward. The reaction force lifts the rocket. The rockets continue firing until the spaceship is traveling fast enough to escape Earth's gravitational pull. Then the spaceship needs far less fuel. Its inertia, or tendency to move forward, is usually enough to keep it moving toward its destination.

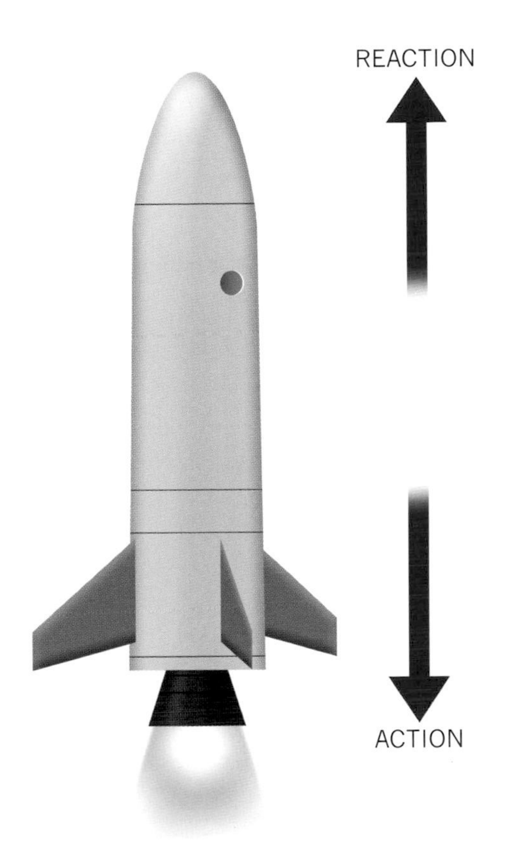

As Newton's third law explains, gases that rush downward lift the rocket upward.

THE DANGER OF ROCKETS

For many years NASA had a record of great success launching manned spacecrafts with rockets. That changed in 1986, with the loss of the *Challenger* space shuttle. Soon after launch, a seal failed inside part of the rocket. This allowed hot gases to escape, and the rocket and shuttle blew apart quickly. The crew of seven astronauts all died.

In 2003 the *Columbia* space shuttle broke apart as it returned to Earth. The cause was a piece of foam that had broken off the shuttle and damaged its heat shields. As with the *Challenger*, all seven astronauts were killed.

The *Challenger* and *Columbia* disasters show the dangers of traveling on rockets. NASA takes great care to inspect all equipment and takes all possible safety precautions. Nevertheless, accidents have happened in the past. They could happen again.

WORD STORE **space shuttle** spaceship that can be used for many missions

Changing direction

Have you ever inflated a balloon, then let it go? As the air rushes out the mouth of the balloon, the balloon quickly zooms around the room. The escaping air is like a rocket engine. The rushing air is the action force (see page 24). The reaction force pushes the balloon in the opposite direction from where the mouth is pointing.

As you may have observed, however, the direction of a speeding balloon can change many times. The balloon could just as easily strike the ceiling as it could strike a wall or the floor. The direction changes because the balloon wobbles or spins as it moves. When the mouth of the balloon points in a new direction, the speeding balloon changes direction, too.

Guiding the rocket

Why doesn't a rocket veer and crash like a balloon? The reason is because it has a guidance system. This system includes movable parts of the rocket, including fins along its side. It also includes instruments that measure the rocket's position and direction, and computers that analyze these measurements.

Older rockets used small rockets next to the main engine. These additional rockets were called vernier rockets. By firing vernier rockets on one side of the main engine, the direction of the rocket could be changed. Other rockets used thrust vanes, which work something like the rudder of a ship to steer the rocket.

In modern rockets, the guidance system can rotate the direction that the rocket engine points. This type of rotation is called gimballing. Gimballing, when properly controlled, makes the rocket's flight especially stable.

Rocket guidance systems

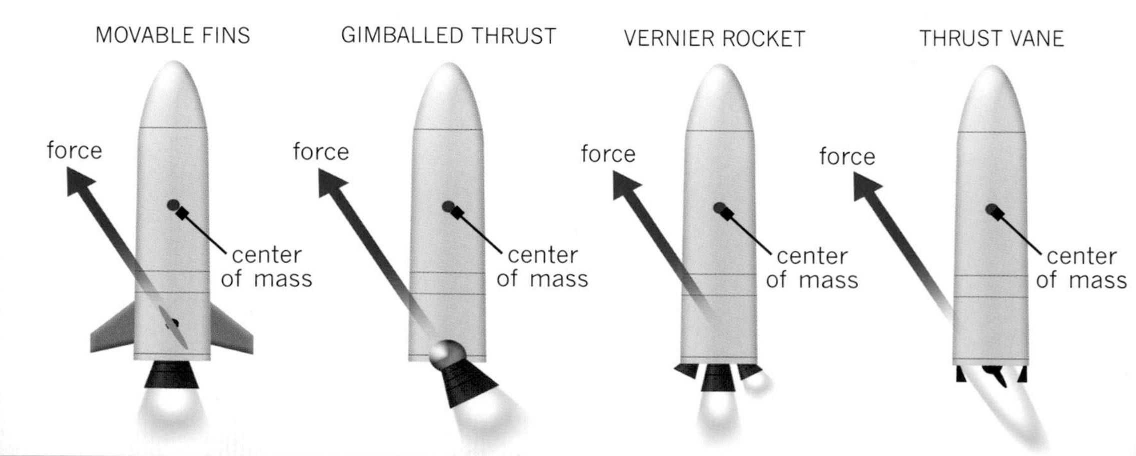

WERNHER VON BRAUN

The work of many scientists contributed to rocket technology. But as most critics agree, the leading rocket scientist was the controversial Wernher von Braun. He is often called the father of rocket science.

Von Braun was born in Germany. He worked to develop rockets for his country before World War II (1939–45). Evidence also shows that he worked for the Nazis during the war. Following World War II, it was illegal for the U.S. government to hire former Nazis. However, von Braun and others were seen as such valuable scientists, that the U.S. government found ways around the problem. When the war ended, the U.S. recruited von Braun and many of his colleagues. Many historians believe that the government altered the scientists' records to remove evidence of their political histories.

Nevertheless, von Braun worked tirelessly, developing rockets first for the U.S. military and then for NASA. His greatest achievement was developing the Saturn rockets that sent astronauts to the Moon. In 1975 he received the National Medal of Science.

Regardless of his politics and beliefs, Wernher von Braun helped the United States send astronauts to the Moon.

Learning from the past

For a mission that sends astronauts to Mars, rocket scientists face a very complex task. A spacecraft must be launched into space, travel to Mars, land on the surface, and then return to Earth. The spacecraft must be large enough to hold astronauts, as well as the air, food, and water that they need to survive. It must also maintain a reasonable temperature.

How could this be accomplished? To begin answering this question, rocket scientists can study a set of missions that completed a similar task. These were NASA's Apollo missions of the 1960s and 1970s. In these missions astronauts traveled to the Moon and returned home safely.

Each Apollo mission to the Moon was designed in much the same way. Three astronauts were launched into space. Their spacecraft had two main modules, or parts, called the command module and the lunar module. When the spacecraft began orbiting the Moon, the modules separated. The lunar module carried two astronauts to the Moon's surface, remained there for a day or so, and then lifted off again. A third astronaut remained in the command module. The modules joined together again to carry the astronauts back to Earth.

Stopping at the depot

In theory a mission to Mars could work in much the same way. Yet many factors make the Mars mission more challenging. For example, each Apollo mission took less than two weeks from liftoff to return to Earth. A mission to Mars would last at least 18 months—and probably longer! For every astronaut aboard, the space capsule would need to carry sufficient food, water, and oxygen.

For these reasons astronauts to Mars would likely need to stop at a kind of "space depot" in orbit around Earth. Supplies could be sent in advance to this station. In theory this would save fuel that the Mars mission would need.

A "space depot" is now under construction. Although it is being built for many purposes, it could be useful for Mars exploration. It is called the International Space Station and will be discussed later in this book (see pages 38–39).

Here is the lander of the Apollo 9 mission as viewed from the command module. Missions to Mars will likely rely on landers and command modules, too.

THE CHALLENGES

Over the past 60 years, **NASA** and other space agencies have chosen many men and women to be astronauts. By all measures their choices have been very successful. The world's astronauts seldom make serious errors on their missions, and none has ever been observed to panic. When accidents have occurred, astronauts have acted bravely and correctly.

Yet a mission to Mars presents many challenges, including its long length. The journey from Earth to Mars would take at least nine months. At least nine more months would be needed to return. Only a few astronauts have lived in space for longer than one year at a time. And none has traveled farther from Earth than the Moon.

Many astronauts might volunteer for a mission to Mars. So might ordinary citizens who lack special training. Who should be selected? The choice could determine whether the mission is a success or a failure.

Safety is a major priority for space missions. Astronaut Mark C. Lee can be seen here testing NASA's Simplified Aid for EVA Rescue system (SAFER). SAFER is a device that allows an astronaut to move around freely in space without floating away.

Dozens of pilots wanted to be America's first astronauts, and these seven were chosen. Today, astronauts are men and women, and they come from all over the world.

The Mercury Seven

In the 1950s NASA began an astronaut search for its first space program. This program was Project Mercury. The goal of Project Mercury was to send an astronaut into **orbit** around Earth, then return the astronaut safely.

At first the scientists in charge of the project viewed the astronaut's role as more of a passenger than a pilot. Nevertheless, NASA considered only test pilots from the U.S. military. Many pilots volunteered, and they were put through months of testing and interviews. Seven astronauts were eventually chosen, all men about 35 to 40 years old.

Astronauts today

Today, astronauts are much more diverse than in the early days of space travel. Astronauts now are men and women, come from many different ethnic backgrounds, and come from places all over the world.

To be accepted for training as a NASA astronaut, candidates must have a college degree in science or mathematics. They must also be in good general health and be neither unusually tall nor short. Pilots and commanders must have experience flying jet airplanes.

Astronauts for Mars

As on other missions, a Mars astronaut would face moments of great stress. The astronaut's special skills certainly would be tested. Yet the many months of space travel would likely be very repetitive and boring.

Imagine looking at the stars every night, but without Earth on the horizon. This is what deep space travel is like.

To conserve fuel the space capsule would need to be small and sparse. The capsule certainly would be equipped with a radio, video monitor, and computer. These devices would provide entertainment and ways to communicate with Earth. For exercise, there might be a treadmill or similar device. An astronaut might be able to leave the capsule, but only when wearing a protective suit and helmet.

EIGHT HUNDRED DAYS IN SPACE

Cosmonaut (Russian astronaut) Sergei Krikalev holds the record for the longest time in space. By the time he retired, he had completed six space missions that together lasted over 800 days. His mission aboard MIR, a space station, lasted almost a year.

Krikalev has earned many medals and awards, among them the Hero of Russia. He also is married and a father. He enjoys swimming, skiing, and other sports.

Krikalev (in the orange space suit) has served with astronauts from many countries, including the United States.

The dangers of space

Can space travel harm an astronaut's health? Yes, it can. Space scientists continue to study ways to keep astronauts healthy and protect them from the dangers of space.

Space is dotted with planets, stars, and other massive objects. Most people think that aside from such objects, space is completely empty. But this is not entirely true.

All parts of space contain trace amounts of gases, including **hydrogen** and helium. In addition, traveling very quickly through space are tiny charged **particles**, such as protons and electrons. The Sun releases these particles, as do other stars. The particles from the Sun are called the **solar wind**.

Earth's protection

On Earth the effect of the solar wind can be seen in places near the North and South poles. Earth's **magnetic field** deflects the solar wind to the poles, where the particles interact with the **atmosphere**. The result is a colorful light show called an **aurora**.

Colorful auroras are common sights in the far north and far south. They form because of Earth's magnetic field.

WORD STORE

aurora colorful lights caused by reactions between solar wind and Earth's atmosphere

Astronauts often enjoy the feeling of weightlessness. On a long space journey, however, bones and muscles can weaken due to lack of use.

Auroras are also a sign of how perfect a place Earth is for life. Without a magnetic field around it, Earth would be bombarded by the solar wind. The particles would cause changes in DNA, the **molecule** used by all living things. These changes likely would lead to cancer and other diseases, much like how sunburns can cause skin cancer.

Staying healthy in space

On a short space mission, an astronaut's health might not suffer from the solar wind or other forms of cosmic **radiation**. On a mission that lasts over a year, however, the risk becomes much greater. Even though astronauts are protected by spaceships and space suits, cosmic radiation can still affect them.

In 2008 British scientists began designing a shield to improve the way a spaceship blocks the solar wind. The shield would deflect the solar wind with magnets, much like the way Earth is protected.

Another health threat for astronauts is the low-gravity environment of space. During the mission astronauts typically enjoy living in low gravity. They can jump up flights of stairs, bounce off of ceilings and walls, and live in other ways that are impossible on Earth. But they also lose bone mass in low gravity. When they return to Earth, they often feel weak and low on energy.

Scientists are studying ways to reduce the health effects of low-gravity life. Creating artificial gravity in space could be part of the answer.

WORD STORE **molecule** set of joined atoms

Training

Imagine that scientists have figured out how to send astronauts to Mars and return them safely to Earth in good mental and physical health. Imagine that rockets are being built, astronauts are being chosen, and all the details of the mission are being carefully planned. Is this all that is needed for a successful mission? No, not entirely. The astronauts must be trained to carry out their duties.

At NASA today, astronaut training begins with two years of studying in classrooms. Trainees study all the science that can affect space travel, including topics in Earth science, life science, and physics. They also learn to use scuba gear to breathe underwater. Like an astronaut in space, a scuba diver must know how to survive away from the atmosphere.

Astronauts are also trained with simulators. A simulator is a machine that mimics, or simulates, a certain experience. NASA has simulators for many of the events that astronauts experience, including lifting off in a rocket and floating weightless in space. After many hours in a simulator, an astronaut knows just what to expect during the real event.

...and practice

Yet training like this is only the beginning. When astronauts are chosen for a mission, they practice every step of the duties they must perform. In 2009, for example, astronauts were sent to perform repairs on the Hubble Space Telescope. To prepare for this mission, they practiced for days on a model telescope on the ground.

Astronauts also practice how they respond to accidents. One of the most famous and dangerous accidents in space occurred during the Apollo 13 mission in 1970, when an explosion caused a loss of electricity and **oxygen**. Because of the training and knowledge of the astronauts on the mission and the scientists on the ground, the astronauts were able to return to Earth safely.

For a mission to Mars, astronauts would surely be trained very thoroughly. The training might last as long as the mission itself, if not longer. Scientists likely would build a "model Mars" using data gathered from space **probes** and telescopes. Many scientists point to desert landscapes on Earth as good models of Martian surfaces. Look back at the photo on page 13. Martian landscapes like this are actually much more Earth-like than any other planet, or even the Moon.

Astronauts often train underwater. Like a deep sea diver, astronauts on a space walk must breathe air from tanks.

The International Space Station

After World War II, the United States and another powerful country, the Soviet Union, became fierce rivals. Space travel was one of the ways they competed, especially during the 1950s and 1960s. Both nations spent huge sums of money on their space programs.

Today, space travel is more expensive than ever before. But rather than competing, the nations of the world have been cooperating with one another. Their biggest project is the International Space Station. When completed, the International Space Station will be the second-largest object in orbit around Earth. (The largest orbiting object is the Moon.)

The station is being built in pieces. Starting in 1998, the pieces have been built on Earth, sent into space, then assembled there. Astronauts and scientists have been living in the station since 2000.

The station's main purpose is scientific research. But in the future, it could serve important roles for long-term space flight. Spacecrafts for travel to the Moon or Mars could be tested there. When the time arrives to launch these missions, they likely would stop at the station to pick up supplies or crew members.

The station may perhaps serve another purpose. It is run by the space agencies of several governments, including the United States, Russia, Japan, and several European nations. In the future other nations may join in the project. If so, the station could unite the world's people to reach a common goal.

Like the International Space Station, a mission to Mars would likely be too expensive for any single nation to support. If many nations joined together to send astronauts to Mars, perhaps all people would feel a part of the mission.

The crew for the International Space Station comes from countries all over the world. So does the station itself.

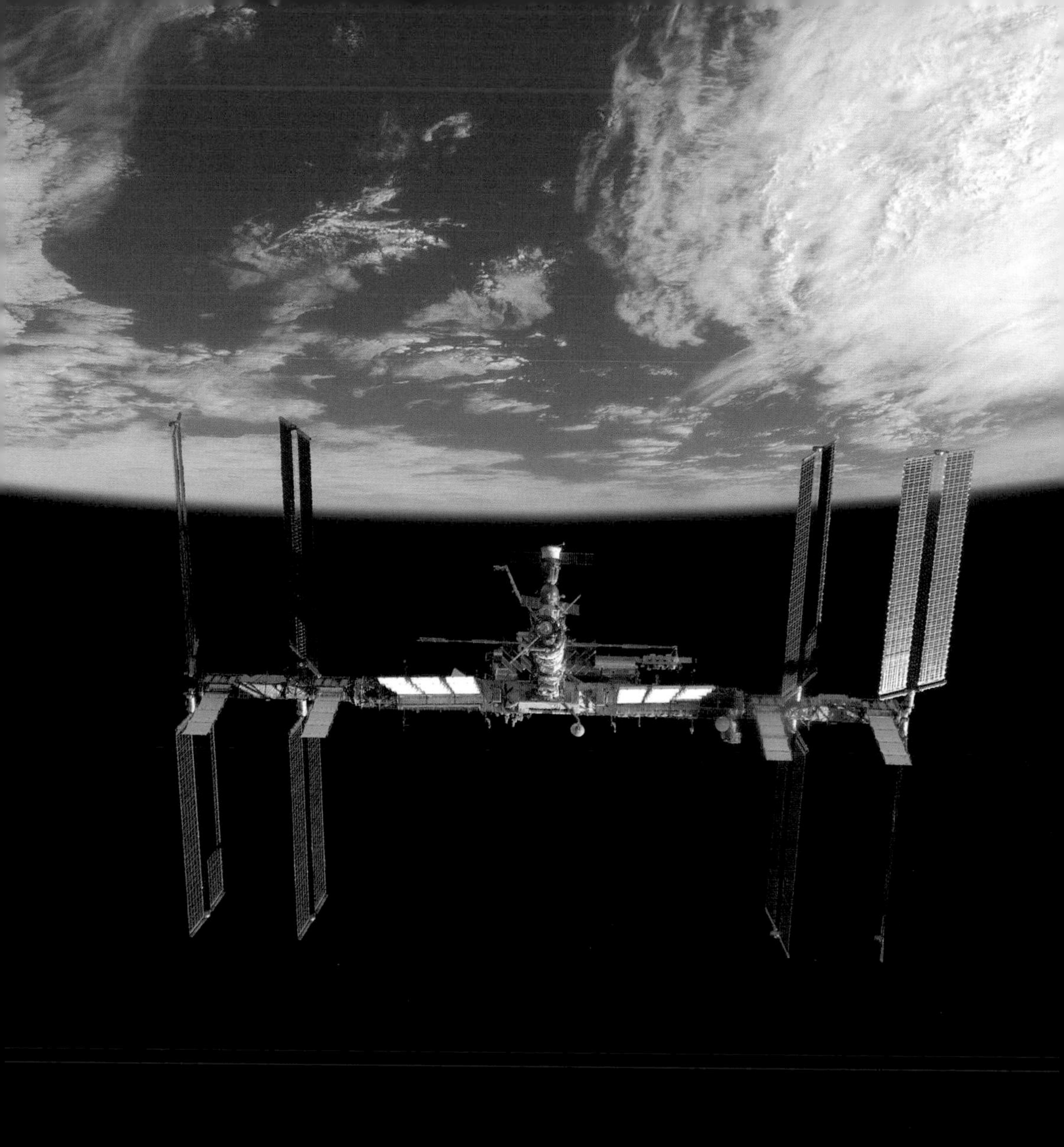

The International Space Station was built in pieces on the ground, then assembled in space. Large solar panels, located on both ends of the station, make electricity for the station from sunlight.

A COLONY ON MARS

Suppose astronauts complete a mission to Mars. What happens next? For an answer, turn back to page 4 and read the quotation from Buzz Aldrin. He urges us not only to visit Mars, but also to build a human colony there.

Many people have imagined what a colony on Mars might look like. The entire colony would probably be under domes and flat buildings of thick glass or plastic. These structures would hold all of the food, air, and water for the colony. They would also protect the colony from the cold temperatures and **atmosphere** of Mars.

The people of the colony could communicate with Earth over radio waves, and spaceships might come and go. But otherwise, they would be living by themselves on another planet. They would be Martians!

Scientists must solve many problems before they can send even one person to Mars. Nevertheless, a colony on Mars is something they can still think about and discuss. You can think about it, too, as you read this chapter.

The biosphere

On Earth, the set of all living things is called the **biosphere**. The prefix *bio* means "life." The living things of the biosphere need many things to stay alive, including water, air, the soil, and the Sun. They also need one another. Animals need plants for food and to make **oxygen**. Plants and animals need tiny organisms in the soil to break down dead materials.

In 1987 a private company built a structure called Biosphere 2 in Oracle, Arizona. The company intended Biosphere 2 to be a small version of Earth's biosphere, as well as a model for a space colony.

As the photo shows, Biosphere 2 looks like a greenhouse. It is surrounded by glass walls and has many plants inside it. But unlike a greenhouse, Biosphere 2 was meant to be sealed shut, or at least to stay shut most of the time.

A new world

Today, living on the surface is one of several models for a colony on Mars. Remember that the air of Mars has little oxygen and is very thin. A colony's buildings would need strong walls to hold the air humans need to breathe. Water would stay inside, too. If the walls were glass, sunlight would shine through during the day, but nothing else would enter or leave very often.

A colony would likely be built in stages. Many missions to Mars would be needed. Each would bring material to build more of the buildings, as well as more air, water, and other supplies. Each mission might also bring more **colonists**.

But a colony on Mars might not be built on the planet's surface. In recent Mars explorations, caves have been discovered. Some scientists are starting to think that these caves could be used to build an underground human colony. Using existing caves for a colony might help solve many of the problems of building on the surface.

Biosphere 2 provides another kind of lesson for a colony on Mars. Since it was built, its owners and mission have changed several times. Air and water now flow in and out of the dome, and people come and go as they like. For people to survive on Mars, their mission could not change so easily. A colony on Mars could not afford to fail.

WORD STORE

biosphere set of all living things on Earth
colonist person who settles in a colony

In 1994, these people agreed to be sealed inside Biosphere 2. Many problems forced the mission to end after six months.

Biosphere 2 was built to model a colony on another planet. Plants inside it provided both food and oxygen.

Things to bring

What must colonists bring to Mars? The following is a list, but it is only a beginning. The list could grow much longer as scientists learn more about Mars and how people could survive there.

Water

On Earth we use water to drink, bathe, water crops, cook, and for recreation. Mars has water, but most of it is frozen in ice caps. Colonists will want to bring as much water to Mars as possible.

Colonists traveling to Mars must bring plants. The Martian soil cannot support plant growth, so the colonists likely will bring soil, too.

SHOULD WE BRING BACTERIA?

Many bacteria cause disease, and they certainly will be unwelcome on Mars. But other bacteria will be essential! Certain bacteria take in nitrogen from the air and change it into a form that plants can use. The process is called nitrogen fixation, and it is the main reason why Earth's plants and animals have the nitrogen they need.

Other soil bacteria help break apart dead organic matter (remains of plants and animals) into usable nutrients. Bacteria in the human intestines help digest food, and others promote healthy skin. So, yes, if humans are to live on Mars, they will need to bring bacteria with them.

Air

Earth's atmosphere is made mostly of **nitrogen** and oxygen, and both gases are important. We can survive without oxygen for perhaps a few minutes at most. Although we do not breathe in nitrogen, compounds of nitrogen are needed to make proteins, DNA, and other essential **molecules** of life.

Plants and soil

Plants make oxygen, and colonists will need to eat food from plants. Plants can be raised in water, a practice called hydroponics. But healthy soil is needed to break down dead plant matter and to fix nitrogen (see box).

Minerals

What do iron, copper, zinc, magnesium, iodine, and manganese all have in common? The human body needs them to stay healthy. These are **minerals**, which are nonliving metals and other materials. We need minerals in very small amounts, and on Earth they usually are easy to find. But that may not be true on Mars.

Electrical generators

The colony will need electricity. Solar cells, which run on sunlight, would be a good way to make electricity on Mars. Nuclear power might also be a good option. **Hydrogen** fuel cells could provide some power as well.

What would colonists need to leave behind on Earth? Pets and farm animals would be on that list. Animals need food to eat, water to drink, and space to live and grow. Very few animals, other than humans, would likely be sent to Mars. Because of this, the colonists would need to be vegetarians.

New pioneers

Someday in the very distant future, people might travel to and from Mars as easily as they fly across the Atlantic Ocean today. But most likely, if you left Earth to live on Mars, you would be leaving Earth forever. The first journeys to send colonists to Mars might be one-way only. Parts of the spaceship could be used to build the colony.

Do you think this idea is frightening? If so, think about some similar stories from history. Beginning in the 1600s, people left the cities and towns of Europe for new lives in the Americas or Australia. Many never expected to see their native countries again, and many never did.

Can we do it?

Could a human colony on Mars grow and succeed? Could it become a place where people would want to live all their lives? The answer depends on many improvements in science and technology. It also depends on whether people could lead useful lives on Mars. Perhaps Mars has useful minerals that could be mined. Perhaps its soil could be made to grow crops. Or perhaps humans could find some other ways to make a home on Mars.

In the 1800s, many Americans traveled across the Great Plains to new homes in the West. Most left their old lives behind them.

TERRAFORMING

Not many people would want to spend all their lives inside a small building. For a colony on Mars to truly succeed, humans would need to change all or part of Mars to meet their needs. In science fiction stories, this is called terraforming. *Terraforming* means changing a planet so that it is more like Earth.

For many years, people have changed Earth's land to suit their needs. We irrigate farmland, meaning we bring water to it. We also add fertilizer to the soil. Under a glass roof, perhaps the Martian soil could also be made fertile (capable of growing things).

On Earth, water and fertilizer can change dry, sandy soil into fertile farmland. On Mars, both the land and air would need to be changed for the same result.

MARS AND BEYOND

Former astronaut Buzz Aldrin was born in 1930. Though no one knew yet, the nations of the world would soon be struggling through hard times. Many people would be out of work and unhappy. A world war was on its way, and it would last for several years.

When Aldrin was your age, not many people were thinking about adventures in space. Yet that quickly changed. At age 39 Aldrin became the second person to walk on the Moon.

Today, **NASA** is sending **probes** to Mars and beyond. Other missions send astronauts to the International Space Station, which is in **orbit** around Earth. But it will be many years before NASA or any space agency is ready to send astronauts to Mars.

When Buzz Aldrin speaks about sending astronauts to Mars, he hopes to convince scientists, government leaders, and the general public. But perhaps most of all, he hopes to convince people your age. Years of work lie ahead before such a mission is possible. The work has already begun, and it will continue only if a new generation of scientists takes up the challenge. Perhaps one of those new scientists will be you.

TIMELINE OF MARS EXPLORATION

1960 The Soviet Union attempted to launch a Martian probe. The launch failed.

1965 Mariner 4 became the first probe to fly by Mars and send images to Earth.

1969 Mariner 6 and 7 sent images of Mars's equator and southern hemisphere.

1976 Viking 1 and 2 became the first probes to land on Mars. They sent many images, but found no signs of life.

1997 Mars Pathfinder brought the first rover to Mars. The rover tested for chemicals and took photos.

1999 Mars Polar Lander reached Mars, but contact was quickly lost.

2003 Rovers *Spirit* and *Opportunity* began exploring the Martian surface and transmitting data. They continue functioning many years longer than originally expected.

2006 Mars Reconnaissance Orbiter began orbiting Mars and studying the atmosphere.

GLOSSARY

atmosphere layer of gases that surrounds a planet

aurora colorful lights caused by the interaction between the solar wind and Earth's magnetic field

bacteria tiny, single-celled organisms

biosphere set of all living things on Earth

climate yearly pattern of weather

colonist a person who settles in a new colony

geology science that studies the physical structure of things, such as planets

hydrogen chemical element, used as rocket fuel in its liquid form

magnetic field effect of a magnet in the region around it

mineral nonliving metal or other nonliving material. Living things need some minerals to survive.

molecule set of joined atoms

NASA (National Aeronautics and Space Administration) agency of the U.S. government that explores space

nitrogen element that exists as a gas in Earth's atmosphere and is used by living things

orbit to circle around a planet; an orbit is also the path taken by something that circles a planet

oxygen gas in Earth's atmosphere that is essential for the life of many organisms, including humans

particle tiny piece of material

probe spacecraft that studies space with equipment, but does not carry astronauts

radar a system for detecting objects using electromagnetic waves

radiation energy given off by atoms as invisible waves or particles

radius a straight line from the center to the edge of a circle or a sphere

rover vehicle that roams across a planet's surface

solar wind particles from the Sun that travel through space

space shuttle spaceship that can be used for many missions

uranium radioactive element used to power submarines and nuclear power plants. It is being considered for rocket fuel.

FIND OUT MORE

BOOKS

Scott, Elaine. *Mars and the Search for Life*. New York: Clarion, 2008.

Simon, Seymour. *Destination Mars*. New York: HarperCollins, 2004.

Siy, Alexandra. *Cars on Mars: Roving the Red Planet*. Watertown, MA: Charlesbridge, 2009.

Strickland, Brad and Thomas E. Fuller. *Mars Year One: Missing!* New York: Alladin, 2004.

WEBSITES

Windows to the Universe
www.windows.ucar.edu
Learn about Mars and other bodies of the solar system.

Exploratorium: Journey to Mars
www.exploratorium.edu/mars
Journey to Mars with the rovers *Spirit* and *Opportunity*.

The Mars Millennium Project 2030
http://mmp.planetary.org
See what a colony on Mars might look like, and who would be part of it.

Astronomy for Kids
www.kidsastronomy.com
Check out the latest news about Mars and other planets in the solar system.

A Timeline of Rocket History
http://history.msfc.nasa.gov/rocketry/index.html
Learn about the first rockets and the rockets of today.

PLACES TO VISIT

Smithsonian Institute
National Air and Space Museum
601 Independence Avenue Southwest
Washington, D.C. 20472

www.nasm.si.edu

TOPICS TO LEARN MORE ABOUT

- ***Beagle 2***
  What happened to the European Space Agency's (ESA) *Beagle 2*, and why did it get its name?
- **Current Moon missions**
  Who's exploring the Moon today? Read up on what's happening with the Chinese Lunar Exploration Program (CLEP).

INDEX